MW01290588

HOW TO MAKE EVERY HOUR IN YOUR LIFE - "HAPPY HOUR"

Author
and
Happiness guru
Jim Gentil

HOW TO MAKE EVERY HOUR IN YOUR LIFE -

"HAPPY HOUR"

Today is the 1st day of the rest of your life and this day is filled with 24 hours. You can make them **Happy Hours** by putting in a little effort, using the right attitude and putting yourself in the right frame of mind.

Follow the simple instructions in this book and I guarantee you will have a happier life and your 24 hours will be a joy to you, your family and those around you.

Author and Happiness guru
- Jim Gentil

INTRODUCTION

From: The State of Texas House of Representatives,
Resolution H.R. No. 1263

WHEREAS, Distinguished speaker, author, and magician Jim Gentil, has positively influenced the lives of people around the world; and

WHEREAS, Mr. Gentil was introduced, in his early years, to the writings of Earl Nightengale's *The Strangest Secret* which led him to become a prominent figure in the field of positive thinking; and

WHEREAS, Publishing his first book, The Sixty Second System of Success, Mr. Gentil has gone on to become a noted writer, motivational speaker, and magician; in January 1998, he began publishing a weekly newsletter titled *Positive People Power! Newsletter*, which has garnered readers from across the United States and 30 different countries; and

WHEREAS, Mr. Gentil is know by many as *"Mr. Positive,"* and he is most deserving of special recognition for helping others to find the bright side of life and to achieve remarkable feats in their own lives; now therefore be it

RESOLVED, That the House of Representatives of the 78th Texas Legislature hereby honor Jim Gentil for his professional success and extend to him warmest best wishes for continued happiness; and, be it further

RESOLVED, That an official copy of this resolution be prepared for Mr. Gentil as an expression of high regard by the Texas House of Representatives.

Remember only **you**
can make **you** happy.

Now read on with Mr. Positive, Jim Gentil and learn
How to Make Every Hour in Your Life – HAPPY HOUR!

WELCOME TO THE 24/7 WORLD
OF PERSONAL HAPPINESS

What you have in your hands is a workbook – use it like you would any other workbook. Mark it up, underline important parts, hi-lite key ideas, tear out pages and tack them up, copy any part and tape it to your mirror or pass it on to others or rewrite parts or phrases to suit you and your personal goals.

Make this book work for you.

Use it on a daily basis. Carry it in your pocket, purse, briefcase, glove compartment or in your lunch container.

Read it in your spare time – waiting for car pools, riding to work (not driving to work), coffee breaks, lunch time, waiting times, stuck in traffic times, delivering kids, picking up kids, bedtime or anytime.

You deserve the results that can be achieved by the use of this book.

You owe yourself the better life that can be yours.

This is your book. Use it as instructed. If it doesn't provide you with ways to change your life for the better, your money will be refunded. A happier life is yours with this book – *HOW TO MAKE EVERY HOUR IN YOUR LIFE – HAPPY HOUR!*

HOW TO MAKE EVERY HOUR IN YOUR LIFE – HAPPY HOUR!

Copyright 2013 by Jim Gentil

For more information:
Contact Positive Winners Press,
P.O. Box 340108, Austin, Texas 78734
Jim Gentil – 512-415-4651

Life is so very short and we never know which day will be our last. So live each day in the fullest way and leave your personal legacy of living a happier life to those you love and cherish.

This book is available at special discounts when ordered in large quantities for promotions, premiums, fund raising or educational use.

If you would like additional information on using this book as a gift for your clients or employees with your logo and information as a sponsor on the cover contact us at **positivewinners@aol.com.**

Table of Contents

You Gotta Have a Sense of Humor

Humor - Each year – and you can start your year today – 4 splendid seasons, which gives you 365 bright mornings and starlit evenings, 12 months full of beautiful possibilities, 52 promising weeks, and – a year to be savored with 8736 hours for you to be happy.

24/7 Happy Hours
Marvelous Monday
Terrific Tuesday
Wonderful Wednesday
Tremendous Thursday
Fantastic Friday
Stupendous Saturday
Super Sunday

Plus More Happy Hours
Incredible Next Day
Sensational Some Day
Awesome Today
Exciting Every Day

You Need the Right Attitude and Right Stuff

Attitude - Learn the Sixty Second System of Success, the How-To for creating positive habits.

Persistence is the Name of the Game

Persistence – Be like the professional athlete. You have to train to be positive.

Your Health is Important – Mind and Body

Health – the ELEMENTARY program to becoming a truly vibrant person. Young at Heart – keeping mind, heart and soul - lively, creative and energetic. Passion - Learn to control stress *and Laugh yourself well* - Switch on and switch off

You are Living Potential

Optimism – the outlook we all want and need to be a success.

Upbeat – the personality and feel you want to achieve.

Rejuvenate – always feeling better and accomplishing more

*****

To succeed in life, you need three things: a wishbone, a backbone, and a funny bone.

- Reba McEntire

*****

While attending a Marriage Seminar dealing with communication,

Tom and his wife Grace listened to the instructor, "It is essential that husbands and wives know each other's likes and dislikes."

He addressed the man, "Can you name your wife's favorite flower?"

Tom leaned over, touched his wife's arm gently and whispered, "It's Pillsbury, isn't it?

You are the same today that you are going to be five years from now except for two things: the way you think and the positive habits you acquire. So acquire the positive habit of making every hour in your life – **Happy Hour!**

You Gotta Have
a Sense of Humor

There was this husband who was in big trouble when he forgot his wedding anniversary.

His wife told him "Tomorrow there better be something in the driveway for me that goes zero to 200 in 2 seconds flat".

The next morning the wife found a small package in the driveway.

She opened it and found a brand new bathroom scale.

Funeral arrangements for the husband have been set for next week.

*****

In May 2006, I was diagnosed with vocal cord cancer. I went through seven weeks of radiation and ten weeks of recovery. For a time I wasn't sure if I would be able to talk again. But I was blessed. So I know the value of a positive attitude, a sense of humor and of making every hour in my life – **Happy Hour!**

Have you ever seen a miracle? Most every time people see a new-born baby, someone says "that's a miracle!"
And someone probably said that about you when you were born and the fact is you still are a miracle.

Think about it for a moment---

How many of you play the lottery???

If you bought a ticket – the odds are usually about 55 million to 1 of winning. But you have already won a much bigger lottery against much greater odds. ***You were born!***

A college study was made to calculate the odds of a specific individual being born.

They estimated the total number of fertile men and women in the world, calculated the number of genetic possibilities a man might contribute, adjusted for the number of hours of female fertility each month, then factored in a long list of other considerations.

The bottom line: the chance that you, meaning exactly you, would ever be born are 1 in 1.3 times ten to the twenty-ninth power.

In other words, 13 followed by 28 zeros.

You and me are some incredibly, amazingly, unbelievably lucky people.

We won the genetic lottery!

So you are a miracle and you already have won a lottery more amazing than humankind can ever devise. You have already been awarded a prize far richer than anything the world has to give. You are alive. You are here. Make the most of it. You are a miracle – so start making every hour in your life – **Happy Hour!**

You Really Do
Needa Sense of Humor

Most all of us are endowed with the five senses...maybe they don't all work too well...but, most of us can see - hear - smell - touch and taste........but what we all really need (if we don't have it) is the *sixth sense*.......the sixth sense is the sense of humor and a sense of humor will help to make every hour in your life – **Happy Hour.**

The *sixth sense* helps you to relieve stress, reduce tension, gives you a good self-image, increases your self-esteem, exercises your insides, and makes you feel good all over.

A true sense of humor is where you laugh at yourself with others rather than laugh at others with others.

A sense of humor will help you over life's hurdles better than any medicine or drug. Laughter is the greatest tonic in the world and it's my drug of choice...and it is kind of like a drug, because laughter releases endorphins which are pain relievers and stress reducers.

To be successful in whatever business you're in, you've got to *STP - see the people.* You've got to go out and show your smiling face to them. And if you don't have a smiling face....then as a college professor of mine once said.....if you don't have a smile and a sense of humor, then you better go out and beg, borrow or steal one...because nothing will help you to succeed more in life than a sense of humor and a smile on your face. You should never leave the house without this important part of make-up on your face.

Learn to laugh often! Because laughter is still just about the best medicine known. Medical science is beginning to research the effects that laughter has upon people's health and have found plenty to smile about.

Studies have revealed that a good belly laugh will help fight infections, stress, hypertension and headaches. A hearty laugh will stimulate your chest, diaphragm, heart, lungs and liver. Your pulse can shoot from 60 to 120 as your blood pressure rises from 120 to 200 as an increased supply of oxygen courses through your bloodstream.

Laughter affects blood pressure both ways. If you have low blood pressure, laughter will raise it. If it's high, laughter will put it back down where it belongs.

In this age of high-tech, scientific miracles and medical break-throughs, it just might be that something as simple as - *laughter is the best medicine* - really. So have a good laugh whenever and wherever the mood strikes you.

*****

LAUGHTER
THE CURE FOR WHAT AILS YOU

Turn That Frown Upside Down

Consider these statistics compiled in a Harvard Medical School study:

Children laugh at least 10 times more often than adults. And pessimists are twice as likely as optimists to develop heart problems, the study said.

Laughing for only 10 minutes a day also has been shown to reduce high blood pressure and arthritis pain.

Laughing 100 times roughly equals 15 minutes on an exercise bike but laughing is easier and you can do it almost anywhere.

Vigorous laughter increases the heart rate deepens the breathing, expands the blood vessels, and more!

Laughter boosts immunity - Infection-fighting antibodies are released into the system.

Statistics On How Laughter Impacts Health
- **Laughter relaxes the whole body.** A good, hearty laugh relieves physical tension and stress, leaving your muscles relaxed for up to 45 minutes after.
- **Laughter boosts the immune system.** Laughter decreases stress hormones and increases immune cells and infection-fighting antibodies, thus improving your resistance to disease.
- **Laughter triggers the release of endorphins,** the body's natural feel-good chemicals. Endorphins promote an overall sense of well-being and can even temporarily relieve pain.
- **Laughter protects the heart.** Laughter improves the function of blood vessels and increases blood flow, which can help protect you against a heart attack and other cardiovascular problems.

Did You Know?

Laughter is contagious - laughter by one person can provoke laughter from others; hence, the laugh tracks that have commonly been added to comedy shows. A long time ago, television companies that were filming live would add people to the audience who were paid to laugh.

The Magic Of Laughter

Laughter is an immediate mood enhancer. It has been well documented that there are positive physical changes that take place in your body when you laugh. **Try feeling bad and laughing at the same time - it can't be done.**

You can choose to laugh or cry in response to just about anything.

Laughing is always easier than crying but you wouldn't want to do it at a funeral or at another inappropriate time. Although, I can remember just after a funeral while visiting with others at the following reception people began sharing their memories of the deceased and many of those memories were particularly funny and endearing. The shared laughter that followed seemed to have a healing quality to it as the deceased was remembered and missed at the same time.

*****

**Laughing with others is more powerful
than laughing alone.**

Creating opportunities to laugh
- Watch a funny movie or TV show.
- Go to a comedy club.
- Read the funny pages.
- Seek out funny people.
- Share a good joke or a funny story.
- Check out your bookstore's humor section.
- Host game night with friends.
- Play with a pet.
- Go to a "laughter yoga" class.
- Goof around with children.
- Do something silly.
- Make time for fun activities (e.g. bowling, miniature golfing, karaoke).

Shared laughter is one of the most effective tools for keeping relationships fresh and exciting. All emotional sharing builds strong and lasting relationship bonds, but sharing laughter and play also adds joy, vitality, and resilience. And humor is a powerful and effective way to heal resentments, disagreements, and hurts. Laughter unites people during difficult times.

Incorporating more humor and play into your daily interactions can improve the quality of your love relationships— as well as your connections with co-workers, family members, and friends. Using humor and laughter in relationships allows you to:
- **Be more spontaneous.** Humor gets you out of your head and away from your troubles.
- **Let go of defensiveness.** Laughter helps you forget judgments, criticisms, and doubts.

- **Release inhibitions.** Your fear of holding back and holding on are set aside.
- **Express your true feelings.** Deeply felt emotions are allowed to rise to the surface.

Laughter is an immediate mood enhancer. It has been well documented that there are positive physical changes that take place in your body when you laugh. **Try feeling bad and laughing at the same time - it can't be done.** You can choose to laugh or cry in response to just about anything.

*****

Laugh yourself Well, It is Time to Distress

We have all heard that laughter is the best medicine. Well, here is some scientific evidence to prove it. According to the American College of Sports Medicine, individuals who watched comedy had better "arterial compliance." Translated into English that means the amount of blood that passes through the arteries is increased. Therefore the 75 trillion cells that make up your body get more oxygen, more nutrients and are overall better fueled when you laugh, all the while helping lower your blood pressure at the same time.

In another study, the long lasting benefits of a little comedy added to life was further documented, "Arterial compliance was improved for a full 24 hours after subjects watched a funny movie," per researcher Jun Sugawara.

So, it seems a laugh a day can help keep the doctor away. It is time to kick back and laugh, rent a movie and de-stress and be well. I strongly believe that stress is a hugely under-appreciated killer, contributing to accelerated aging and premature death. If you have not evaluated your stress levels, it is time to do so.

To start on the pathway to making every hour in your life – **HAPPY HOUR,** you need to become more aware of your true sense of humor. The difference between a plain sense of humor and a true sense of humor is in the ability to laugh at your self. With a plain sense of humor, you laugh at others. But with a true sense of humor, you laugh at things that happen to you – with others.

How do you go about acquiring this new, true sense of humor and with it a new self-image, (if you don't already have it.) Well, first you have to learn how to smile and I mean smile **Big!**

SMILE
IT'S ONE OF THE BEST THINGS
YOU CAN DO WITH YOUR FACE.

One Sunday morning, I went to a 7/11 to get some milk for breakfast.
The clerk said, "Do you need a bag for that?".
I said, "No."
She said, "Well, I need a smile!"

That incident made me think on the value of a smile and how it affects our attitude and others. A smile on your face the first thing in the morning can help to make your day more alive and exciting.

It would be great if we could tattoo a smile on our faces...

HOW A PENCIL CAN MAKE YOU SMILE!

However, you say you can't smile – well let me teach you a way to practice smiling. Years ago, two groups of people were asked to judge how funny they thought *The Far Side* cartoons were and then rate how happy they felt.

One group was asked to hold a pencil between their teeth, but to ensure that it did not touch their lips. The other group supported the end of the pencil with just their lips, but not their teeth.

Without realizing it, those in the "teeth only" position had forced the lower part of their faces into a smile, while those in the "lips only" position had made themselves frown.

The results revealed that the participants experienced the emotion associated with their expression. Those who had their faces forced into a smile felt happier and found *The Far Side* cartoons much funnier than those whose faces were forced to frown.

The message from this work is simple – if you want to cheer yourself up, act like a happy person. If need be, <u>fake it till you make it.</u>

Right now, put a SMILE on your face and hold it for 20 seconds and you will start to feel better. Also other people will want to know what the heck you are smiling about!

So get yourself a pencil and practice smiling. Look in the mirror to see how it really does work.

SO YOU NEED TO ADD A SMILE TO YOUR FACE!

* People seldom notice old clothes if you wear a big smile. - **Lee Mildon**

* A smile is a curve that sets everything straight. ~**Phyllis Diller**

* Smile. Have you ever noticed how easily puppies make human friends? Yet all they do is wag their tails and fall over. ~**Walter Anderson**

* Before you put on a frown, make absolutely sure there are no smiles available. ~**Jim Beggs**

* A smile is an inexpensive way to change your looks. ~**Charles Gordy**

* Wrinkles should merely indicate where smiles have been. ~**Mark Twain**

* A smile is the light in the window of your face that tells people you're at home. ~**Author Unknown**

* If you smile when no one else is around, you really mean it. ~**Andy Rooney**

* If you smile at someone, they might smile back. ~**Author Unknown**

* Life is like a mirror, we get the best results when we smile at it. ~**Author Unknown**

* Always remember to be happy because you never know who's falling in love with your smile. ~**Author Unknown**

* Everyone smiles in the same language. ~**Author Unknown**

* If you don't have a smile, I'll give you one of mine. ~**Author Unknown**

* I've never seen a smiling face that was not beautiful. ~**Author Unknown**

* Wear a smile and have friends; wear a scowl and have wrinkles. ~**George Eliot**

* Smile - sunshine is good for your teeth. ~**Author Unknown**

* If you don't start out the day with a smile, it's not too late to start practicing for tomorrow. ~**Author Unknown**

- **Laughter boosts the immune system.** Laughter decreases stress hormones and increases immune cells and infection-fighting antibodies, thus improving your resistance to disease.

- **Laughter triggers the release of endorphins,** the body's natural feel-good chemicals. Endorphins promote an overall sense of well-being and can even temporarily relieve pain.

- **Laughter protects the heart.** Laughter improves the function of blood vessels and increases blood flow, which can help protect you against a heart attack and other cardiovascular problem

* Smiling is my favorite exercise.
~Author Unknown

* I have a tickle in my brain. And it keeps making the corners of my mouth point toward the heavens.
~Jeb Dickerson

* Wear a smile - one size fits all.
~Author Unknown

* Every day you spend without a smile, is a lost day. **~Author Unknown**

* Every time you smile at someone, it is an action of love, a gift to that person, a beautiful thing. ~**Mother Teresa**

* Keep smiling - it makes people wonder what you've been up to. ~**Author Unknown**

* You're never fully dressed without a smile. ~**Martin Charnin**

* A smile can brighten the darkest day. ~**Author Unknown**

* All the statistics in the world can't measure the warmth of a smile. ~**Chris Hart**

* If you would like to spoil the day for a grouch, give him a smile. ~**Author Unknown**

* Smile - it increases your face value. ~**Author Unknown**

* Peace begins with a smile. ~**Mother Teresa**

* A smile is a powerful weapon; you can even break ice with it. ~**Author Unknown**

* Most smiles are started by another smile. ~**Author Unknown**

* A smile is something you can't give away; it always comes back to you. ~**Author Unknown**

A smile costs nothing but gives much. It enriches those who receive without making poorer those who give. It takes but a moment, but the memory of it sometimes lasts forever. None is so rich or mighty that he cannot get along without it and none is so poor that he cannot be made rich by it. Yet a smile cannot be bought, begged, borrowed, or stolen, for it is something that is of no value to anyone until it is given away. Some people are too tired to give you a smile. Give them one of yours, as none needs a smile so much as he who has no more to give.

The Benefits of Laughter

Physical Health Benefits:	Mental Health Benefits:	Social Benefits:
*Boosts immunity	*Adds joy and zest to life	*Strengthens relationships
*Lowers stress hormones	*Eases anxiety and fear	*Attracts others to us
*Decreases pain	*Relieves stress	*Enhances teamwork
*Relaxes your muscles	*Improves mood	*Helps defuse conflict
*Prevents heart disease	*Enhances resilience	*Promotes group bonding

It takes a lot of work from the face to let out a smile, but just think what good smiling can bring to the most important muscle of the body... the heart.
~**Author Unknown**

*****

Amazing simple home remedies:
these really work!!

1. To avoid cutting yourself when slicing vegetables, get someone else to hold the vegetables while you chop.

2. To avoid arguments with the females about lifting the toilet seat- use the sink.

3. For high blood pressure sufferers ~ simply cut yourself and bleed for a few minutes, thus reducing the pressure on your veins. [remember to use a timer.]

4. A mouse-trap placed on top of your alarm clock will prevent you from rolling over and going back to sleep after you hit the snooze button.

5. If you have a bad cough, take a large dose of laxatives - you'll be afraid to cough.

6. You only need two tools in life - wd-40 and duct tape. If it doesn't move and should, use the wd-40. If it shouldn't move and does, use the duct tape.

7. If you can't fix it with a hammer, you've got an electrical problem.

ALL PEOPLE SMILE IN THE SAME LANGUAGE

One group of people, who use the mirror method to get their adrenalin up, are the disk jockeys of America. Many of them have mirrors in from of them and before they open the microphone to talk, they smile, put on a happy face and then pass their enthusiasm on to the listeners.

This process is also used by most all telephone sales people and by most anyone using the telephone to sell any type of product, because happy, smiling faces produce energetic, upbeat voices that produces good feelings that sells products.

Grumpy, negative voices don't sell. Listen to your favorite radio station and listen to the positive, vibrant sounds that come from the announcers and how they make you feel.

During my tenure as disc jockey/news director at a small market radio station many humorous events took place because of the fun atmosphere that prevailed there. Many disc jockeys took immense delight in trying to break me up as I read the news. Most were extremely successful, as my Seriousness Tolerance Level is very low. They would set fire to the news I was reading, turn out the lights, pour water down my back, moon me or even worse, undress me – all while I was reading the news.

This all helped me to develop my sense of humor and to work at making every hour in my life **– Happy Hour!**

You Need the Right Attitude
and Right Stuff

Now that you know how to *Smile*, we can begin with learning how to develop a Positive Attitude.

My neighbor had a dog that he kept outside on a cable run between two giant shade oak trees. Daily he released him for a little taste of freedom. But the dog never realized he was free, for he would continue to run back and forth between the same two trees as if he was still on the chain.

Do you keep running back and forth between your same trees, not realizing your freedom to change and become the person you were meant to be. Remember it's never too late to be the person you've dreamed of becoming. You can make every hour in your life – **Happy Hour!**

*****

TO HELP YOU CREATE A POSITIVE MINDSET –
I DEVELOPED A PROGRAM CALLED...

THE 60 SECOND SYSTEM OF SUCCESS

The 60-SSS is a simple system to understand and for any program to be successful it must be simple.

It's like the guy who went to Australia and saw a platypus at the zoo. When he returned home he want to order a couple of them for the local zoo. But he didn't know the plural of platypus – whether it was platypies, platypees or platypussies.

So he began to write,

Dear Sir, Please send me a platypus and while you're at it, send me another one.

He made it simple to understand and he was successful.

However, even though this system is simple and simple to understand, you do need to put forth some effort.

My 60-Second System of Success **will enhance your self-esteem, give you an attitude of positive expectancy and help you TO RELIEVE NEGATIVE STRESS in your life today and everyday and make every hour in your life – Happy Hour!**

In the 60-SSS, I give you a plan of action...I give you a time frame for completion...and ask you to give yourself...a commitment to achieve a better life for you and your family.

We need to train our minds with this program to be happy and we can do this by following the working the process which includes the three ways of learning – visual (seeing), – auditory (hearing) – kinesthetic (feeling).

First...the plan of action... invest 60 seconds a day

1. *FIRST THING IN THE MORNING.*

I ask you to look in the mirror and smile..........

How many of you look in the mirror and see: a successful, energetic, happy, enthusiastic, positive, high-achiever person.........

Or do you see: a down-trodden, negative, frowning, stressed-out, unhappy person.

Think about it, when you wake up and look in the mirror - what do you see?
Positive or Negative
Happy or Sad

REMEMBER WHAT YOU SEE IS WHAT YOU GET!!!

So if you smile and repeat the power affirmations, then you release endorphins, which gives you a natural high.

Start each day looking in the mirror with a big smile on your face - because what you see is what you will get! You are in control of your feelings. So be **HAPPY!**

THE FIRST 15 SECONDS
UPON ARISING

Look in the mirror and **SMILE** and repeat the
affirmations and use the signs, so that you are using
your seeing, hearing and feeling senses.

Affirmations	**Success Signs**
I feel fantastic I feel great I feel super I feel terrific I feel wonderful	thumbs up
I'm number one I like myself I love myself	# 1 - index finger up
I'm at peace with my self	peace sign - index and middle fingers
I'm the best I'm the greatest and this day I am achieving my goal, because I'm a positive powered winner	victory sign arms raised in <u>v</u> overhead
and winners say *"YES!"*	arm pump

SMILE
AND REPEAT THE POWER
AFFIRMATIONS

Remember it's not what others say to us...

It's what we say to ourselves when they stop talking. We start telling ourselves the negatives about ourselves. If someone says, "that's a stupid thing you just did," our mind starts telling us, "well, maybe that was stupid and maybe I am stupid."

Always tell yourself the positives – I am not stupid and I don't do stupid things. I am a winner and I believe in myself. They don't know me as well as I know myself.

Look in the mirror again with a big smile on your face - remember what you see is what you get! Repeat the affirmations and use the signs.

THE SECOND 15 SECONDS

SMILE - Repeat the affirmations and use the signs, so that you are using your seeing, hearing and feeling senses.

Affirmations	**Success Signs**
I feel fantastic I feel great I feel super I feel terrific I feel wonderful	thumbs up
I'm number one I like myself I love myself	# 1 - index finger up
I'm at peace with my self	peace sign - index and middle fingers
I'm the best I'm the greatest and this day I am achieving my goal, because I'm a positive powered winner	victory sign arms raised in **v** overhead
and winners say *"YES!"*	arm pump

QUESTION???

HOW MANY OF YOU FOR THE FIRST TIME TOLD YOURSELVES - I LIKE MYSELF – I LOVE MYSELF.

We don't tell ourselves *I like myself* and *I love myself* enough. We need to always tell ourselves the positives. Don't ever tell yourself negatives – other people will take care of that for you.

THE THIRD 15 SECONDS

3. *IN THE EVENING...*

Look in the mirror again **SMILE** - Repeat the affirmations and use the signs, so that you are using your seeing, hearing and feeling senses.

Affirmations	**Success Signs**
I feel fantastic I feel great I feel super I feel terrific I feel wonderful	thumbs up
I'm number one I like myself I love myself	# 1 - index finger up
I'm at peace with my self	peace sign - index and middle fingers
I'm the best I'm the greatest and this day I am achieving my goal, because I'm a positive powered winner	victory sign arms raised in <u>v</u> overhead
and winners say *"YES!"*	arm pump

YOU CAN USE AFFIRMATIONS TO LOSE WEIGHT

* Maybe you don't need to lose weight. You may be like me, I have a beautiful body, but I keep it hidden inside this one.

* There's a new method to determine whether or not you need to lose weight. It's called the 30-30 method. What you do is jump up and down for 30 seconds and if there is anything still jiggling after the next 30 seconds, you might need to lose some weight.

* I grew up in a large family and we didn't always have a lot to eat. So what my mother did was to give us beans for breakfast-water for lunch-and at suppertime we'd just swell up.

*****

THE FOURTH 15 SECONDS

4. *PASS ON TO OTHERS*...with kind words and/or gestures.

During the day tell others they look fantastic, great, super, terrific, and wonderful. Compliment others with nice suit, great tie, your dress, etc. Any type of compliment is a win-win situation. You feel good complimenting someone and you feel good when you receive a compliment.

So pass on your good thoughts with a pat on the back, a hug, and of course, a **SMILE**.

QUESTION?

* When do you tell your spouse or significant other that you love them, *before somebody else does.*
* I spoke to a group of retirees one time, and said the line above.

After my program, a lady came up to me and told me that when if said, "when do you tell your spouse you love them, before somebody else does," her husband turned to her and said, "I love you."

I told her "that's nice".

She said, "No you don't understand, we've been married 42 years and that's the first time he told me he loved me."

* Did you hear about the man who didn't kiss wife for 20 years, but then shot guy who did.

* Everyday hug and kiss your family and tell them you love them.

THAT'S THE PLAN OF ACTION...
SMILE AND REPEAT
THE POWER AFFIRMATIONS
3 TIMES A DAY
FOR 15 SECONDS
AND PASS IT ON WITH A KIND
WORD/GESTURE TO OTHERS FOR THE
OTHER 15 SECONDS.

NOW THE SECOND PART...

Second...
the time frame for completion

I'm asking you to do this for 30 days, because it takes almost 30 days for anything to become a habit in your life. A good example is moving a waste-basket from one side of your desk to the other side. It will take you almost 30 days before you quit throwing paper on the floor where the waste-basket had previously been.

IF YOU WILL DO FOR 30 DAYS WHAT MOST PEOPLE WON'T DO...THEN YOU CAN DO FOR THE REST OF YOUR LIFE...WHAT MOST PEOPLE CAN'T DO.

REMEMBER IT'S NEVER TOO LATE TO BE WHAT YOU COULD HAVE BEEN !

So work the program for 30 days. And just like athletes, you have to train yourself to achieve your goals, dreams and wants.

If you repeat the POWER AFFIRMATIONS for 30 days, they will become a part of your life.

The system works. You cannot think negative if you're smiling.

Try to think of a negative thought........

now **SMILE** .....

it releases endorphins and the negatives disappear.................

*****

"Most folks are about as happy as they make their minds up to be." ~*Abe Lincoln*

"Smile. Actions speak louder than words. A smile says ....I like you – you make me happy, I'm glad to see you, glad to hear from you." ~*Dale Carnegie*

"A dog's way to smile is by wagging its tail." ~*Unknown Author*

"We come into this world crying while all around us are smiling. May we so live that we go out of this world smiling while everybody is weeping." ~*Persian Proverb*

"Laughter is a smile with the volume turned all the way up." ~*Unknown Author*

"In every job, relationship, or life situation, there is inevitably some turbulence – learn to laugh at it. It is part of what you do and who you are." ~*Allen Klein*

SECRET TO BECOMING A MASTER.

If you want to be a master at anything.
Study what the masters have done before you.
Learn to do what they have done.
Have the guts to do it.
And you will be a master just like them.

Because schools don't teach you to be successful, they teach you to fit in.

Third
the Commitment

I've given you the plan of action and the time frame. Now you need to make the commitment to help yourself be the person you've always wanted to be. We all have areas of our lives that we would like to change....

HERE IS YOUR CHANCE.

Plan of action...Time Frame for Completion...Your Commitment.

At the beginning, I said the 60 SSS was simple to understand, but required some effort on your part. It takes your motivation to make the commitment a reality. And I can't give you what you already have. I can explain this simple system to you...but the motivation and commitment must come from within.

Make a strong, definite commitment to follow through on becoming a positive powered winner! Make the words - passion, discipline, persistence, desire and determination - a part of your everyday vocabulary.

TRAINING PROGRAM
FOR CREATING POSITIVE SELF-ESTEEM

One of the most important tools in becoming a success in life - is our own mind - we become what we think about. If we think about success - we will become successful. But, if we think we are going to fail - we will fail.

When I was graduating from college I happened into the college bookstore and came across a 33 1/3 RPM record (that was before cassettes, CD's, I-pods and MP3's) called *"The Strangest Secret"* by Earl Nightengale.

I had never heard of Earl Nightengale before, and little did I know how he would influence the rest of my life.

He had a six-word philosophy that has guided my whole life - the six words – *"you become what you think about"* - and through the years before others had said the same thing

King Solomon, in chapter 23, verse 7 of Proverbs, says, *"as a man thinketh in his heart, so is he."*

Shakespeare said, *"nothing is either good or bad, but thinking makes it so."*

and Henry Ford said, *"whether you think you can or think you can't - you're right!"*

and then Earl Nightengale said it in six words - *"you become what you think about."*

The late Dr. Norman Vincent Peale, tells the story of going by a tattoo shop in Hong Kong and of seeing the many different designs available to be inscribed on the body. He saw eagles, dragons, hearts and many other assorted slogans and inscriptions. He then noticed one that said, "born to lose." Dr. Peale wondered why anyone would want such a negative idea etched on their body so he asked the owner if anyone had chosen that particular tattoo. The owner said only a few had chosen that one and then added *"tattoo on mind, before tattoo on body."*

So we need to tattoo and train our minds to be happy and we can do this by following the following program. We learn three ways – visual (seeing), – auditory (hearing) – kinesthetic (feeling). This uses our senses of learning.

This training program is the 60 Second System of Success. You cannot become a success in 60 seconds, but it teaches you to develop a single positive habit and if you can develop one – then you can develop as many positive habits in which you are willing to invest your time.

Start each day looking in the mirror with a big smile on your face - remember what you see is what you get! Repeat the affirmations and use the signs.

Make a strong, definite commitment to follow through on becoming a positive powered winner!

*****

POSITIVE PEOPLE POWER! TIPS

* Put affirmations on fridge,
* On bathroom mirror,
* In your wallet,
* On your computer,
* On your ceiling for you to see when you go to bed and when you wake up, In your desk drawer, so when you open the drawer the words are there for you to see,
* On your phone and/or Ipad device.

*Hang up positive saying all around your office, garage, den, kid's rooms, laundry room and wherever they can be a positive reminder to you. Remember you are in training to make every hour in your life – **HAPPY HOUR** and if you do these things, you will soon see your attitude and mood changing to being fully charged with energetic feelings of joy, happiness, fun, and a more active, enthusiastic lifestyle.

Think of yourself as a product:

* Write a commercial selling you as the product.
* What are the qualities that would make people want to buy you?
* List the benefits people would receive as a result of buying you.

> Joy dishwashing soap,
> Land o' Lakes ice cream,
> Lexus automobile,
> Burger King, …etc…

Be creative !!! Use humor, if appropriate.

Another way to jump start your positives is to sing the following songs to yourself.

From the movie, Oklahoma –
O what a beautiful morning,
O what a beautiful day,
I've got a wonderful feeling,
Everything's going my way.

From the movie, Song of the South –
Zip-A-Dee-Doo-Dah, Zip-A-Dee-A
My oh my what a wonderful day
Plenty of sunshine headed my way
Zip-A-Dee-Doo-Dah, Zip-A-Dee-A

And from the songwriter, Johnny Mercer -
You've got to accentuate the positive,
Eliminate the negative,
Latch on to the affirmative,
And don't mess with mister in-between.

You know you can tell someone you love them
a hundred times and they may not believe you,
but tell someone you hate them once
and they will never forget it.

*****

You need the right attitude!

YOU ARE IN CONTROL OF YOUR ATTITUDE
– OTHERS AFFECT YOUR ATTITUDE, BUT
YOU CONTROL YOUR ATTITUDE. YOU ARE
IN COMPLETE CONTROL OF YOUR
REACTION TO ANY SITUATION OR WORDS
THAT ARE SPOKEN TO YOU!

Laugh often, Dream big, Reach for the stars!
Nobody ever died of laughter.
~ Max Beerbohm
-
"Laughter is the shortest distance
between two people"
~Victor Borge

Laugh as much as you breathe
and love as long as you live.

Persistence is
the Name of the Game

Constancy of purpose
is the first principle of success.

It is critical to your success that you have a well-thought-out plan for your life and that you stick with it regardless of what others may say and the obstacles you encounter.

There will always be fault-finders and those who attempt to persuade you that your goals aren't worth the effort you're putting into achieving them. Those people will never go far, and they will be the first to ask for your help after you have passed them by.

Virtually every successful person has considered giving up at some point in his or her struggle to reach the top. And many breakthroughs occurred soon after those same people rededicated themselves to their purpose.

There is no known obstacle that cannot be overcome by a person who has constancy of purpose, a Positive Mental Attitude, and the discipline and willpower to succeed.

IF YOU WANT A THING BAD ENOUGH

If you want a thing bad enough to go out and fight
for it,
To work day and night for it,
To give up your time and your peace and your sleep
and for it;
If only the desire of it makes your quite mad enough
never to tire of it;
If life seems all empty and useless without it,
And all that you dream and you scheme is about it;
If gladly you'll sweat for it, fret for it, plan for it,
Lose all your terror of God and man for it;
If you'll simply go after the thing that you want with
all your capacity,
Strength and sagacity; faith, hope, and confidence,
stern pertinacity;
If neither poverty nor cold nor famish nor gaunt
Nor sickness or pain to body or brain can turn you
away
From the thing that you want;
If dogged and grim, you besiege and beset it,
you'll get it!
- **Berton Braley**

WHAT IS PASSION ?

* it's having a purpose or passion for what you want to achieve in life
* it's your goals, desires, wants
* it's being active with family, work, networking group or whatever is of great interest to you.
* it's you wanting to know how to get whatever you want –
* it's establishing a goal worth working for.
* better still, get yourself a project.
* just to be continuously working is not enough. Always have something ahead of you, to "look forward to", to work for and hope for.
* always visualize your next step.
* keep moving after you achieve a goal and set another.
* momentum is maintained by always having something to look forward to.
* constantly give yourself something to work for.
* do what you can do well, and do well whatever you can do.
* **do whatever it takes, goals are what keep you going.**

GREAT THOUGHT

If you will spend and extra hour each day of study in your chosen field – you will be a national expert in five years or less. This is possible because no one else is doing it.

Switch On Switch Off

This is a mental exercise that will teach you and prepare you to take charge of your thoughts. It can be done anywhere. Practice makes perfect. Take a few moments to rest, breathing in and out.

- Think calming thoughts (ocean waves, fly fishing, having a massage, anything that is calming)
- Now switch to a funny thought (a funny TV show, a time that made you giggle, a happy moment)
- Switch your thoughts again to an angry thought (a time when someone took advantage of you, a time when you were treated rudely)
- Switch back to the calming thought
- Repeat the process

Think of a remote control that you switch to different channels.

As you go through the process become aware of how you are in control. Notice how you have the power to change your thoughts and in turn your emotions. The more you practice this technique the more effective you will become at changing your state of mind when you really need to.

Laughter gives us distance.
It allows us to step back from an event, deal with it and then move on.

* Even if there is nothing to laugh about, laugh on credit.

* She laughs at my dreams, but I dream about her laughter.

* A good laugh and a long sleep are the best cures in the doctor's book.

* Laughter is the way to true love.

* A man isn't poor if he can still laugh.

* Laughter is a medicine with no side effects.

* Laughter means sympathy.

* Laughter is the shock absorber that eases the blows of life.

* Laughter is a tranquilizer with no side effects.

* Laughter is part of the human survival kit.

* What soap is to the body, laughter is to the soul.

* Laughter is the closest thing to the grace of God.

* Laughter is not at all a bad beginning for a friendship, and it is far the best ending for one.

* Remember, men need laughter sometimes more than food. - **Anna Fellows Johnston**

* Laughter is by definition healthy. - **Doris Lessing**

* Laughter on one's lips is a sign that the person down deep has a pretty good grasp of life. - **Hugh Sidey**

* Perhaps I know best why it is man alone who laughs; he alone suffers so deeply that he had to invent laughter. - **Friedrich Nietzsche**

* With the fearful strain that is on me night and day, if I did not laugh I should die.- **Abraham Lincoln**

* Laughter is the corrective force which prevents us from becoming cranks. - **Henri Bergson**

* Laughter is the sensation of feeling good all over and showing it principally in one place. - **Josh Billings**

* Seven days without laughter makes one weak. - **Mort Walker**

* Laughter is the closest distance between two people. - **Victor Borge**

* Laughter and tears are both responses to frustration and exhaustion. I myself prefer to laugh, since there is less cleaning up to do afterward. - **Kurt Vonnegut**

ways laugh when you can.
t is the cheapest medicine

some ways the experts say are the best
ir sense of humor.

Situations – Look for the fun and
ryday events. That's what most
comedians do. They take a normal or serious-
sounding situation and exaggerate it to make you
laugh.

* Build a Laugh Library – Collect your favorite
jokes, cartoons, comic strips, CD's, DVD's, movies,
home movies, etc., etc., etc.

* Take a Break – Everyday take 5-10 minutes to
spend in your Laugh Library to enjoy and rise
above the problems of the day.

* Share Your Sense of Humor – By sharing a good
funny story with others you will experience a
special sense of joy only that moment can bring.

*Develop an appreciation of fun, humor and
laughter. It can make life easier to live and makes
you a more enjoyable person to be around.

The following are a few ways to increase the humor in your everyday life. They're practical and easy-to-do, so long as you're serious about using humor to improve your health and general well-being.

-- Collect funny cartoons, jokes, bumper stickers, and anything else that triggers your laughter. Then:

- Place them in a "Funny File" for future reference when you're in need of a laugh; or stick them up in the most stressful places in your house (e.g. your desk, cupboard, mirror, or dressing table)

- Join mailing lists that send jokes every day.

-- Create a journal in which you write any funny encounters that made you laugh.

-- Set aside at least half an hour each week to watch a sitcom, comedy show, comedy movie, etc.

-- Become aware of any comedy clubs in your neighborhood that you could visit; make it a bi-monthly event with a group of friends.

-- Make sure you genuinely laugh at least once a day. (Your girlfriend's new haircut doesn't count.)

-- Exaggerate your tough situations; this helps you see their absurdity. You are given a different perspective, are able to laugh at it, and then you can let go of your problem and move on with your life.

- Look out for any irony in your life: when you end up so far from where you started or from where you wanted to be, empower yourself to find it laughable. To appreciate the irony, you need to examine how something started and how it ended.

Fun idea is to take slogans from one company and apply to other companies.

Example: Maxwell House Coffee slogan matched to Otis Elevator – Good To The Last Drop.

- BONUS: ALWAYS KEEP A SMILE ON YOU TO GIVE TO SOMEONE WHO NEEDS ONE!

Your Health is Important
– Mind and Body

Physical – that's eating right and exercise.

* I tell people that I have a beautiful body, but I keep it hidden inside this one.

* There's a new method to determine if you need to lose weight or not. It's called the *30/30 method*. You jump up and down for 30 seconds and if there is anything still jiggling after the next 30 seconds, you might need to lose weight.

* I made a goal and commitment in 2008 to walk 25 days a month. I walk two miles a day and have walked over 300 days each year for the past 5 years. You can make a commitment to exercise at least 30 minutes a day doing whatever exercise is good for you.

* With good health, you'll feel better, look better, save money on medications and Dr.'s visits. It's a win-win situation.

* So just follow my elementary program and you will have a healthier life and lifestyle and it's easy to do.

ELEMENTARY

Eat
  Less
   Exercise
    More
     Eliminate
      Negatives
       Talk
        Affirmatively
         Remarkable
          YOU

For those of you who watch what you eat... here's the final word on nutrition and health. It's a relief to know the truth after all those conflicting medical studies:

1. The Polish eat a lot of sausage and suffer fewer heart attacks than the Americans.
2. The Mexicans eat a lot of fat and spicy food and suffer fewer heart attacks than the Americans.
3. The Japanese eat a lot of rice and noodles and suffer fewer heart attacks than the Americans
4. The Italians drink excessive amounts of red wine and eat large amounts of pasta and suffer fewer heart attacks than the Americans.
5. The Germans drink a lot of beer and eat lots of sausages and fats and suffer fewer heart attacks than the Americans.

Conclusion: eat and drink what you like. Speaking English is apparently what kills you

Besides physical health
there is also mental health.

Do You See What I See?

Have you ever had an experience where you felt like you were watching yourself interact with someone? It was almost like you were sitting in a studio watching a show. Sometimes, when people experience that they think "Why am I doing that? Why am I saying that?" But they do not take it to the next level, taking charge of themselves and changing. Now you can.

During conversations today observe yourself interacting with others. Watch yourself as though you are watching a show. Observe how you stand, how you are speaking and the tone of your voice. Observe the words you are using. What facial expressions are you exhibiting?

Later on, spend a few moments reviewing the 'show' you just watched. What did you observe about yourself? What did you like? What would you change? How can you improve?

Continue to observe yourself. Begin to make minor changes during your next conversation. Change yourself to be more like the person you want to be. This self-correcting will result in more positive and productive reactions.

This is a powerful tool that will not only change yourself, but change how others react to you. You may perceive it as though they changed, when in fact it was you who changed.

HUMOR QUOTES

* My doctor is wonderful. Once, when I couldn't afford an operation, he touched up the x-rays. - **Joey Bishop**

* I am a marvelous housekeeper. Every time I leave a man, I keep his house. - **Zsa Zsa Gabor**

* If you look like your passport photo, you're too ill to travel. -**Will Kommen**

* Insanity doesn't run in my family. It gallops. - **Cary Grant**

* Every day I get up and look through the Forbes list of the richest people in America. If I'm not there, I go to work. - **Robert Orben**

* Misers aren't fun to live with, but they make wonderful ancestors. -**David Brenner**

* My therapist told me the way to achieve true inner peace is to finish what I start. So far I've finished two bags of M&Ms and a chocolate cake. I feel better already. - **Dave Barry**

* If you love something, set it free. Unless it's chocolate. Never release chocolate. - **Renee Duvall**

* The most remarkable thing about my mother is that for 30 years she served us nothing but leftovers. The original meal has never been found.
 - **Calvin Trillin**

* I haven't spoken to my wife in years. I didn't want to interrupt her.- **Rodney Dangerfield**

* My grandmother was a very tough woman. She buried three husbands and two of them were just napping. - **Rita Rudner**

* My husband wanted one of those big-screen TV's for his birthday. So I just moved his chair closer to the one we have already. - **Wendy Liebman**

* I love deadlines. I like the whooshing sound they make as they fly by. - **Douglas Adams**

* I have an aunt who married so late in life that Medicare picked up 80 percent of the honeymoon.
- **Don Reber**

* I hate housework - you make the beds, you do the dishes - and six months later you have to start all over again. - **Joan Rivers**

* My grandmother is over eighty and still doesn't need glasses. Drinks right out of the bottle.
- **Henny Youngman**

Look For The Silly Side Of Life
Daily Reminder To Reap The Daily Benefits of
Humor: look for the silly side of life. For example,
I can't walk into a store and see the sign "wet floor"
without smiling and laughing inwardly. That's
because it reminds me of a Joan Rivers joke about
her boyfriend who sees the sign "Wet Floor" and
immediately does! Hope you got that. I did say
silly didn't I? Even if you just chuckle, your worries
tend to melt away.

*****

*Stress can be one of the biggest obstacles to long-
term achievement.*

1. Invest thirty minutes in vigorous physical
   exercise, three to five times per week
   (assuming your doctor doesn't have a
   problem with that.) Work up a sweat.
2. Learn relaxation techniques.
3. Cut down on caffeine.
4. Eat right. Savor your food. Understand that
   eating is as much a sensory experience as it
   is a physical necessity.
5. Meditate. Get still. "Center." Go to your
   retreat regularly. You'll find you have more
   control and perspective on your everyday
   world when you return.
6. Develop better time management habits.
   Focus on one thing at a time. When you
   give matters your full attention, they can be
   completed with more satisfaction.

7. Play. Have fun. Recharge. Avoid stressed people. Their stress patterns tend to rub off.
8. Get plenty of sleep.
9. Smile more. Laugh. Use humor to lighten your emotional load.
10 Count your blessings - daily. Make thankfulness a habit. Acknowledge your positive actions and feelings everyday before retiring. Make a habit of reminding yourself that you're a success.
11. Say nice things when you talk to yourself.
12. Simplify.
13. Set personal goals. Give yourself a sense of purpose.
14. Forgive. Grudges are too heavy to carry around.
15. Practice optimism and positive expectancy. Hope is a muscle - develop it.
16. Be still. Let the world rush by you for a few moments. It isn't necessary – or possible – to be in constant motion.
17. Listen rather than interrupt. Why commit your energy to hindering or trying to finish another person's thoughts? Be an active listener – it'll unclog blocked communication channels.
18. Relax everyday with books, television, etc. Give your mind the freedom to roam regularly.
19. Take regular time off. Refresh your mind and body by getting away from routines when they become too restrictive.

20. Live one day at a time. You can drastically increase frustration levels by living in the future or the past.

You are Living Potential

So learn to actively stretch your potential.

What is potential? the dictionary says - capable of being or becoming possible, as opposed to actual

We all have potential – however – some people have more than others.

Watch the one ahead of you, and you'll learn why he is ahead. Then emulate him. One of the surest ways to achieve success is to observe the actions of successful people, determine what principles they regularly employ, and then use them yourself.

The principles of success, as Andrew Carnegie said, are definite, they are real, and they can be learned by anyone willing to take the time to study and apply them. If you are truly observant, you will find that you can learn something from almost everyone you meet. And it isn't even necessary that you know them. You may choose great people who are no longer alive. The important thing is to study their lives, and then learn and apply in your own life the specific principles these people used to achieve greatness.

FIVE STEPS TO BUILDING YOUR PERSONAL BELIEF SYSTEM:

1. Take steps outside of your comfort zone each day. If you are not doing things in your business that scare you a little or a lot - then you are not stretching yourself far enough.

2. Hang out with positive and motivated people - avoid negative people at all costs.

3. Read books and listen to CD's on self-help and success.

4. Have a mentor or coach that helps you move to the next level of success.

5. Build an alliance of supportive friends, family and business associates and stay in touch often.

*****

Seeds of Thought

A thought "magnetized" with emotion may be compared to a seed, which when planted in fertile soil, germinates, grows, and multiplies itself over and over again, until that one small seed becomes countless millions of seeds of the same brand!

However, because life is the way it is, there are probably three kinds of people reading this book today.

- those who will take notes – remember what's said – make a plan, stretch their potential, take action and then become happier and successful.
- then there are those who will take notes remember some of what's said – make a plan, but take no action and no action means no success.
- and then there will be those of you who won't remember what happened here today at all.

I'm not critizing any of you – but the facts prove that because of diverse backgrounds – diverse attitudes – diverse motivation – many of you will never attain your goals, hopes, dreams and ambitions.

My goal is to awaken in you – your dynamic, unlimited potential to be and do any thing you want to become a success in life. You all have potential – and you need to focus on your potential instead of your limitations.

Because many people die from terminal potential.

Sometimes to stretch your potential you just have to sit back and ask yourself some questions about who you are, where you are going, what you want to accomplish, etc.

The following questions may force you to take a moment to do just that.

1. If I had an hour of free time a day, how would I spend it?

2. Who are my heroes and why? Am I anyone's hero?

3. Can I see things from a different perspective? When did I last walk in someone else's shoes?

4. Could I push myself harder at home and/or at work? Could I stand to ease up a little?

5. What 25 things do I want to accomplish before I die?

6. If I could start my life over again knowing what I know now, what would I do differently? What would I not change?

Most of us will never know our true capacity for achievement because we never challenge ourselves to perform at our best every day. We don't stretch our potential.

This truism becomes apparent when you are presented with an opportunity that really interests you.

No matter how busy you may be, somehow you will find the time to pursue it.

Conversely, duties that have little appeal for you are easily postponed and eventually forgotten.

Busy people are not procrastinators.

They know that life, as John David Wright once observed about business, "is like riding a bicycle. either you keep moving, or you fall down."

The most effective people have a sense of urgency.

They set deadlines and force themselves to establish priorities.

Even if your activities don't usually require strict deadlines, set them for yourself.

You will be amazed at how much you can accomplish in a short time -- if that's all the time you have.

The old saying - if you want a job done promptly and well, get a busy person to do it. The idle one knows too many substitutes and shortcuts.

"The only time you do anything different in your life is when you're happy or sad. You never do anything if you're comfortable."

Every problem has in it the seeds of its own solution. if you don't have any problems, you don't get any seeds. - **Norman Vincent Peale**

Pick up an acorn, what will you see.
Some, an acorn; others, a tree.
Squirrels eat acorns because they don't know
If they plant acorns, oak trees grow.

How does an acorn know what it'll be?
Each knows it's meant to be a tree.
What can we learn from a little acorn?
Each has his potential the day he's born.

Your potential is God's gift, he gave only to you.
When you find it and live it, to yourself, you'll be
true.
If that's true, many people ask,
Why is finding your potential such a difficult task.

Yet from the day you were born you were told what
you should.
You looked to others for what you ought and you
could.
So don't look to others for your potential outside.
Look within where your potential resides.

Then live your potential, you will be in control.
You will know your identity, you will own your
soul.

*****
"A cheerful heart is a good medicine."
- Proverbs 17:22

SPIRITUAL ASPECT
OF MAKING EVERY HOUR – HAPPY HOUR

To quote the Bible..."as you sow, so shall you reap." Take this opportunity to start sowing new seeds in your life.

"If you have faith as small as a mustard seed, you can say to this mountain, 'move from here to there' and it will move. nothing will be impossible to you." - Matthew 17:20, NIV

    A mustard seed is a power-packed package of possibilities and potential. Plant this tiny seed in fertile ground and it will grow to be a plant large enough for the birds to build nests in and lay their young. In turn, this plant will produce a plethora of other seeds, which in turn will grow into large plants producing more seed. The potential in one seed is staggering!

Prayer:
    Lord, show me WHAT seed you want me to sow today. Show me WHERE you want me to sow today. Reveal to me HOW to nurture the seed so that it will grow into the dream you planted in my heart - an impossible dream to me, but a possible dream through You! Amen.

What seed have you been called to sow? You might think it is just a tiny seed, not worthy of even a second thought. But don't underestimate the power of your God-given seed. What will the world miss if you think it is not worthy of sowing?

The potential in you is likewise staggering! Only God knows the positive ripple effect of your being used by him. Don't limit him by your perceived limits - lack of experience, education, or financial backing. With God, all things are possible!

A grandfather, a poor, uneducated farmer in Iowa, planted a figurative mustard seed one day when he prayed for a son who would be a minister.

The answer to that prayer was a baby boy who became a minister - Robert Harold Schuller - who has preached to millions around the world.

What seed have you been called to sow? What will the world miss if you, thinking your seed is not worthy, fail to plant that seed? What might the world gain if you plant it?

From Spark To Flame

When my daughter was in Grade 3, all of Mrs. Mathews' students were given a small pot with a bean seed to plant. Green string beans it seems are pretty hardy and the perfect seed to use when promoting green thumbs in young children. That same plant was also a most unexpected source of understanding and insight for me.

Once the bean plants had sprouted and flowered, their teacher allowed the kids to carefully transfer the precious cargo from school to home. Once home, Shanna scouted around for the perfect location and settled on a sunny south window-sill and then proudly declared, "Soon I can feed the whole family!"

Shanna's sisters were envious and even our cat looked intrigued which should have been a warning to me because when I woke up the next morning, I saw that the bean plant had been maliciously knocked off the window sill and ripped from it's pot. Its leaves were frayed and except for a limp thread of stem that still connected the roots to the flowering top, it was quite unrecognizable from the day before. The plant, it seemed, was a goner.

I dreaded what I had to tell Shanna but as I gently began to explain that the bean plant had to be put in the compost, her reaction was not what I expected. She said, "Everything will be okay Mom, the plant will get better."

Without wasting a second in thought she secured the first aid kit from the bathroom returning with gauze, a tongue depressor, bandages and a deep belief that the pathetic looking, near-dead bean plant would live, thrive and even produce food!

I had mixed emotions knowing that she was postponing the plants inevitable trip to the compost bin but I went along with it and helped her wrap bandages. Days later, to my absolute surprise, the bean plant was standing tall and looking perky.

We were able to remove the bandages and discover a protruding hump in the stem where its near-fatal stem break had been. It was also amazing to see that the one and only bean, had become plump almost completely masking the claw marks that had scarred it.

I don't know why I hadn't thought the cat might go for a second round because it surely did, and this time I ran for the first aid kit! I carefully applied a heavy blanket of everything from cotton and gauze to colored band-aids with "ouch" written on them and when the medic work was done, I whispered a little something to the heavens.

Just one week later we were able to take the bandages off and again we barely found evidence of an attack and there was even a new sliver of green where a second bean was forming. I was excited and amazed while Shanna had been expecting nothing less. Back to the window-sill it went but this time we built a fortress of heavy books to keep it safe until our day of bounty.

I set the table beautifully with all the fanfare of a Thanksgiving dinner. The beans were carefully divided by 5, which awarded each person 2 small pieces, claw marks and all. They turned out to be the best green beans I had ever eaten!

My daughter never quite understood my exuberance over the significance of the beans. In my work as a youth motivator I am brought together with kids and teens that all desperately need people to believe in them. Now, more than ever, no matter what I have been told about a child or a teen and their behavior, I see everyone, no exceptions, with the same eyes and heart that my daughter used on her broken, beaten up bean plant.

I wonder if it's a coincidence that later that same week, I stumbled upon a most appropriate quote by Italian Poet Dante (1265-1351): "From a little spark, may burst a mighty flame."

Especially if you believe...! - - **Author Unknow**

God can do powerful things through a tiny seed.

Thoughts to get you through almost any crisis:

* Nostalgia isn't what it used to be.
* Sometimes too much to drink isn't enough.
* Things are more like they are today than they have ever been before.
* It's hard to be nostalgic when you can't remember anything.

Most of you have probably heard the statement that success is a journey and not a destination.

And most of us plan extensively for any journey we take...in fact, I bet most of you planned in some way what you would have for breakfast and where you might have for lunch and who you'd have lunch with, made a mental plan or checked your planner of the activities you'd do at work today, planned what you would do after work or this weekend.

There are powers inside of you, which, if you could discover and use, would make of you everything you ever dreamed or imagined you could become. - *Orison Swett Marsden*

And that's how it is in life - we make plans for taking a vacation; we make a list for grocery shopping, we buy life insurance and plan for death.

Most of our planning consists of someday I'll do this and someday I'll do that, or when this happens then I'll do this... when I turn 18...when I graduate from high school...when I turn 21...when I finish college...when I get that job...when I get married...when I have a family...when they grow up...and on and on and on.

But very few of us really plan our success journey.

Most of us don't have an economic or financial plan, a plan for living a healthy life or a plan for achieving success in life.

And unfortunately, the only person we have to blame for that is ourselves, because we are truly in control of our lives and we are not living up to our potential.

A 60-year-old hotel in Kansas is being renovated into apartments. A rusty ship that is docked in Philadelphia is being restored and may become a hotel or a museum. Hangar 61, an admired piece of architecture at the old Stapleton airport in Colorado, is being transformed into a church. Each structure had a specific use that is no longer viable. Yet someone was able to see promise and a new purpose in each one.

If structures can find new life and purpose, why not people? You can find new life and purpose by stretching your potential.

Whatever you wish to accomplish, there's no reason why you cannot start right now. When you're truly committed to reaching your goal, there will always be something that can be done right away, to get started. Action will get you where you want to go. Excuses will hold you back. The choice is yours. What are you waiting for?

**MAKE EVERY HOUR IN YOUR LIFE –
HAPPY HOUR!**

I recently stopped in traffic behind a large truck. I'm sure you have all seen the numbers displayed on the truck's rear door asking the public to call a certain number if the truck driver was not obeying the rules of safe driving. Most trucking companies displaying such signs surely have confidence in their drivers and their training.

I thought how would my behavior change if I was required to wear a sign requesting that my bad behavior be reported.

Would I be less likely to show frustration because of poor service? Would I be more patient while waiting in line or sitting in the doctor's office? Would I forgive more easily when others made comments that hurt my feelings?

Perhaps I would offer to help a person in need more readily if I were wearing a sign that declares my goal in life.

What will your actions reveal about you today?

Here are a few "small things" you can do:

At work – Add a few hours each month to your professional development outside of the work day knowing that you'll have invested the equivalent of a full work week during the year in your most valuable asset … you.

As a Manager – Act with the understanding that your management role has an objective of developing and encouraging others to succeed by doing the right tasks at the right time … every day … every week … every month … to become the best they can possibility be.

As a friend – Choose to visit or talk with two extra friends each week and create more than 100 additional discussions among friends for the year.

*****

I ask audiences this question: What were worried about this time last year?

I get a lot of laughs because most people can't remember.

Then I ask if they have a current worry - I see nods from everybody.

Then I remind them that the average worrier is 92% inefficient – because only 8% of what we worry about ever comes true."

Why do your think most people are not interested in making every hour in their life – **Happy Hour?**

It may be hard to believe yet two people can have similar childhoods and experience the same thing, yet get different results.

A story about identical twins can show that we can create our lives with our thoughts and the choices we make. Their father was an alcoholic. One became an alcoholic, the other did not. When they were asked why one became an alcoholic when the other didn't, these were their answers.

The alcoholic said he learned to be an alcoholic at his father's knee. He said, as a child he saw his father drink when he was happy and drink more heavily when he was stressed out and upset. He said he must have decided as a child to follow in his father's footsteps.

Yet when the sober twin was asked why he wasn't an alcoholic he answered, "I learned to be sober at my father's knee." That amazed many people because that was what his brother said.

But the sober twin would continue, "You don't understand. Yes, I saw the same things my brother saw. As a child I saw my father drink when he was happy and drink more heavily when he was stressed out and upset." But he continued, "But the next day, I saw him so sick he would throw up, he had terrible hangovers and he spent all the family money on drink and I decided as a child I'd never be like him."

So you might agree we have a choice to be happy or sad or let other people's opinions and behavior influence how we act and feel. I know it may seem hard to be immune to the opinions of others, but when you know deep down that what you are doing and feeling is right for you, it gets easier every time you control your feelings and choose to feel good.

*****

"They say a person needs just three things to be truly **happy** in this world: someone to love, something to do, and something to hope for."
- Tom Bodett

"This life is yours. Take the power to choose what you want to do and do it well. Take the power to love what you want in life and love it honestly. Take the power to walk in the forest and be a part of nature. Take the power to control your own life. No one else can do it for you. Take the power to make your life **happy**." – **Susan Polis Schutz**

"The reason people find it so hard to be **happy** is that they always see the past better than it was, the present worse than it is, and the future less resolved than it will be" – **Marcel Pagnol**

Money can't buy Happiness,
but Happiness can make Money.

"Can money buy happiness?" This is one of the favorite topics between people to discuss. No one can say that they've never talked about this topic.

1. I'm happy because I have a lot of money
2. I'm happy because I have enough money
3. I'm happy because I have more money than others
4. I'm happy because I have a lot of money to do whatever I want.

So, what is your answer? Which one of the above determines the relationship with money and happiness for you?

Unless your answer is the first one, your happiness doesn't have a direct relation with money. In the first answer, just holding a lot of money in your hands, makes you happy. In that case, you can really buy happiness with money.

In other answers, money is only, one of the tools that can help you to be happy. You are not happy because you have money. You are happy because of the results, besides in most cases, you can have these results without money as well.

People who give the second answer are generally happy when their needs are answered. They are grateful for what they have and they are happy with this and they don't expect more than enough.

That is the reason of their happiness. They already know how to be happy with what they have, without the help of money.

People who give the third answer are happy because they feel they have a higher social status than others. This makes them feel successful, powerful and happy. In some cases, it is not only about the social status, it is about helping people. When you have more money, you can help people more and people begin to trust you that, you can be a solution when they need. If this is the case, that means, it is not money what makes you happy, to be trusted and sharing with others is the reason of your real happiness. Read the post: How is trust linked with happiness.

People who give the fourth answer are happy with their freedom and social life. In that case, it is not money, again. Social life or being free can make you happy. It's not the money what you need. Your freedom or social life makes you happy. Where does money stands here? You can buy some spare time to be with your friends. You can get a nanny, hire an assistant or outsource a part of your work to have time with your friends. It's the social life which makes you happy, not the money.

Money always affects your happiness indirectly. On the other hand happiness directly affects your economical success. As money is something material that you can have with your mind power, you should focus on mind power and use money as a tool to improve it. Read the post: money sign.

Money is more related with life satisfaction then happiness. You can be more satisfied with your life when you have all the money you need to do whatever you want. Happiness on the other hand is much more complicated because it depends on different positive emotions and behaviors.

Contrarily, you cannot earn more money unless you are happy. Happiness is the key of success and money. Happiness can bring everything that is positive in your life. You feel like everything is possible when you are happy. You are wide open to opportunities. You don't hide yourself at the back of black clouds. You welcome life as it is, so you can discover novel ways to have money. Your happiness attracts people who can offer you new opportunities to have money.

At the end, you'll be surrounded with countless ways to have money.

Although money cannot buy happiness in long term, happiness can bring money to your life till the end.

Remember Only **You** can make **You** happy.

You know we all start out as fertilized eggs.
How we end up is up to us –
Are you scrambled, fried, boiled, poached, over easy, or sunny side up?

How much have you accomplished is the wrong question sometimes –
Instead we should ask ourselves, if we have hugged a friend, taken a walk, read a novel, or told a joke.
If we long for the past and dream about the future – we will surely miss the present.
I have traveled all over the world and for the most part I have always had good weather.
In many instances, people have asked me "did you bring the good weather with you?"
I'm sure you've been ask that question yourself.
I've thought a lot about it and I believe we all bring weather with us wherever we go.
You always bring a mental climate no matter where you travel.
You step into a room, you meet people, you talk and you either bring sunshine or gloom, shadow or sparkling enthusiasm.
You create a mood wherever you go.
That mood you create and produce is a mental climate that others live with.
You must manage your moods or your moods will manage you.

So how do you feel today? Did you bring this weather with you? Most likely you did!

Morning prayer - Good Morning, God! Thank you for your beautiful world! I want to make your world even more beautiful. So may my face be like happy sunshine and not a dark cloud.

When you meet someone and ask them – " how 's it going?" How do they answer?

Well, there's a list on a scale of 1 to 10 that you should be aware of how the responses rate –

1. Silence or tears
2. Awful – stop the world and let me off
3. Not too bad
4. Pretty good
5. OK
6. Good
7. Great
8. Terrific
9. Super
10. Fantastic

How do you normally respond? Remember a smile is one of the best things you can put on your face.

"You are today where your thoughts have brought you. You will be tomorrow where your thoughts take you." ~ **James Allen**

Attitude Determines Altitude

Unlike some things in life, we can choose out outlook. Sometimes we just need a reminder that happiness can often simply be a result of choosing attitudes;

I woke up early today, excited over all I get to do before the clock strikes midnight. I have responsibilities to fulfill today. My job is to choose what kind of day I am going to have.

Today I can complain because the weather is rainy or I can be thankful that the grass is getting watered for free.

Today I can feel sad that I don't have more money or I can be glad that my finances encourage me to plan my purchases wisely and guide me away from waste.

Today I can grumble about my health or I can rejoice that I am alive.

Today I can lament over all that my parents didn't give me when I was growing up or I can feel grateful that they allowed me to be born.

Today I can cry because roses have thorns or I can celebrate that thorns have roses.

Today I can mourn my lack of friends or I can excitedly embark upon a quest to discover new relationships.

Today I can whine because I have to go to work or I can shout for joy because I have a job to do.

Today I can complain because I have to go to school or eagerly open my mind and fill it with rich new tidbits of knowledge.

Today I can murmur dejectedly because I have to do housework or I can feel honored because I have been provided with shelter.

Today stretches ahead of me, waiting to be shaped. And here I am the sculptor who gets to do the shaping. What today will be like is up to me.

I get to choose what kind of day I will have!

- Author Unknown

Try to make at least one person happy every day, and then in ten years you may have made three thousand, six hundred and fifty people happy, or brightened a small town by your contribution to the fund of general enjoyment. **- Sydney Smith**

Hang in there! In just two days tomorrow will be yesterday. **- Unknown**

Conclusion

To keep you on the right track, keep this thought:

A sense of humor is probably the most essential ingredient you will ever need for a successful and happy life. It is necessary for your mental, physical, and emotional health. It can enrich your relationships, help you raise well-adjusted offspring, boost your career up to the next level, aid communication, make you feel happy, keep you healthier, and even save your life.

Recommended Readings

59 Seconds – Change Your Life in Under a Minute
- **Richard Wiseman**

Choosing Happiness – Keys to a Joyful Life
- **Alexandra Stoddard**

Handbook to a Happier Life – A Simple Guide to Creating the Life You've Always Wanted
- **Jim Donovan**

Happy This Year – The Secret to Getting Happy **Once and For All - Will Bowen**

Lighten Up – Survival Skills for People Under Pressure - **C.W. Metcalf and Roma Felible**

The Light Touch – How to Use Humor for Business Success - **Malcolm Kushner**

The Smile Connection – How to Use Humor in Dealing with People
- **Esther Blumenfeld and Lynn Alpern**

Smile for no good reason – Simple Things You Can Do to Get Happy NOW - **Dr. Lee Jampolsky**

A Whack on the Side of the Head – How to unlock our mind for innovation. - **Roger von Oech**

A Kick on the Seat of the Pants – Using your talents to be more creative. - **Roger von Oech**

Another way to make every hour in your life – Happy Hour is to book me for a Happy Hour presentation to your group, organization or association. The program is filled with fun, laughter, enjoyment, pleasure, and magical *entertainment.

So why do many groups hire me:
Because Jim –
* Has delighted thousands of audience members for over 25 years.
* Has entertained in 35 states and in Asia, Europe, North America, South America and on cruise ships.
* Author of books to help you be more successful - *Sixty Second System of Success*, *Positive People Power!* and *Words to Live By.*
* Was honored in the Texas Legislature with a resolution recognizing Jim as "Mr. Positive," for his efforts as a prominent figure in the world of positive thinking.
* Offers customized programs to fit your needs and wants.

Satisfied Client Comments
I asked Jim to speak at our March luncheon, and after the standing ovation, I knew we had found a great individual to speak and educate our members. I cannot even begin to put into words the flood of emails, phone calls and comments I received from attendees about how delightful, inspiring and absolutely hysterical Mr. Positive is.
Laura Mitchell, President
Lake Travis Chamber of Commerce

Mr. Jim Gentil recently spoke at the bi-annual DADS All-Staff Conference in Abilene, Texas. In fact, not only did "Mr. Positive" speak, he wowed the crowd with amazing feats of magic, and captured their interest and imagination with his message. Jim kept everyone's attention from start to finish with his stories, his insight and his wit.
- Mindy Wright, Supervisor

"The feedback from your session was very good. Here are some of the comments:
* Set goals -- write them down
* A day to balance -- it's not always about work!
* Real life examples
* Humor
* The whole concept of being in control and being positive
* Thanks for putting Deity in the work place
Thanks for sharing your time with us, I know that we needed to hear your message and it has made a difference." - Judi Hovde – Target Corporation

"Jim Gentil, brought the attendees to their feet during the closing session of the Volunteer and Combination Officers Symposium when he spoke about having a positive attitude and how it can help individuals get through the tough times."
John Buckman – National Fire Chiefs Association

"Please allow me to extend a huge "Thank-You "
on behalf of the Hospital Heroes Team here at
Driscoll Children's Hospital. Your lighthearted
humor, incredible magic, uplifting stories and
positive message was a real treat! I know almost
every person is looking forward to more positive
tips for a happier and fulfilling life!"
Robin Smith – Director of Guest Services
Driscoll Children's Hospital

**If your group or organization has program
needs, consider Jim Gentil's variety of programs
designed for keynotes or banquet speeches. All
are designed to increase personal productivity
for individuals and organizations.**

<u>Give Jim a Call</u>
<u>You'll be glad you did</u>

Check out his demo video:
http://www.youtube.com/watch?v=Rt9llem5Q9I

**Add more positives to your life by
signing up for the FREE newsletters!**
Positive People Power! **newsletter is published
every Tuesday and is filled with motivational
and inspirational stories, quotes, poems and
thoughts to help you rekindle your enthusiasm
for living and to empower you to achieve your
dreams and become a success in life. Read in all
50 states and over 30 countries around the
world.**

Positive Spiritual Living! provides a look at your life by giving you a deeper sense of your inner soul. It stresses exercising your faith in all aspects of your life for greater fulfillment.

To sign up - go to the website or email me.
Email: <u>Jim@jimgentil.com</u>
Web: jimgentil.com

Is too much to do and not enough time to do it - causing stress and anxiety in your life.
Do you want the freedom to relax and enjoy life?
Do you want to relieve the pain, inconvenience and frustration of everyday living?
Do you really want to make every hour in your life – Happy Hour?

How to Make Every Hour in Your Life – Happy Hour by adding the following to your daily routine.

HUMOR – comedy, wit, the funny side, hilarity
ATTITUDE – outlook, manner, stance, position, mind-set
PASSION – fervor, excitement, enthusiasm, zeal, delight
PERSISTENCE – determination, diligence, perseverance
YOUNG AT HEART – childlike thinking and action

HEALTH – fitness, wellbeing, strength, vigor, shape
OPTIMISM – cheerfulness, confidence, happiness
UPBEAT – positive, cheerful, optimistic, buoyant, jovial
REJUVENATE – invigorate, revive, refresh, renew, restore

This is a manual shows you how to achieve happiness by getting a sense of humor, acquiring a healthy life style and stretching your potential and making every hour in your life – **Happy Hour!**

Jim Gentil is not listed in America's **"Who's Who"**...he is listed in America's **"Who's He?"**
He has entertained executives of many of the **unfortunate 500 companies,** as well as many **low-ranking government officials.** He has appeared on stages across the U.S. as well as on TV, radio, movies, **(home movies, that is)** **Facebook, Linked In, Twitter** and **You Tube.**
In fact, he has been named one of the best speakers in the country...**not too good in the city**...but **plenty good in the country.**
Now, here he is...the man of the week...**which shows you what kind of week it's been – Jim Gentil**

EXTRA HAPPY HOURS!

"Most folks are about as happy as they make their minds up to be." - *Abe Lincoln*

"Smile. Actions speak louder than words. A smile says ….I like you – you make me happy, I'm glad to see you, glad to hear from you." - *Dale Carnegie*

"A dog's way to smile is by wagging its tail." - *Unknown Author*

"We come into this world crying while all around us are smiling. May we so live that we go out of this world smiling while everybody is weeping." - *Persian Proverb*

"Laughter is a smile with the volume turned all the way up." - *Unknown Author*

"In every job, relationship, or life situation, there is inevitably some turbulence – learn to laugh at it. It is part of what you do and who you are." - *Allen Klein*

Laughter is your birthright, a natural part of life that is innate and inborn. Infants begin smiling during the first weeks of life and laugh out loud within months of being born. Even if you did not grow up in a household where laughter was a common sound, you can learn to laugh at any stage of life.

Begin by setting aside special times to seek out humor and laughter, as you might with working out, and build from there.

Eventually, you'll want to incorporate humor and laughter into the fabric of your life, finding it naturally in everything you do.

Here are some ways to start:

- **Smile.** Smiling is the beginning of laughter. Like laughter, it's contagious. Pioneers in "laugh therapy," find it's possible to laugh without even experiencing a funny event. The same holds for smiling. When you look at someone or see something even mildly pleasing, practice smiling.

- **Count your blessings.** Literally make a list. The simple act of considering the good things in your life will distance you from negative thoughts that are a barrier to humor and laughter. When you're in a state of sadness, you have further to travel to get to humor and laughter.

- **When you hear laughter, move toward it.** Sometimes humor and laughter are private, a shared joke among a small group, but usually not. More often, people are very happy to share something funny because it gives them an opportunity to laugh again and feed off the humor you find in it. When you hear laughter, seek it out and ask, "What's funny?"

- **Spend time with fun, playful people.**
  These are people who laugh easily–both at
  themselves and at life's absurdities–and who
  routinely find the humor in everyday events.
  Their playful point of view and laughter are
  contagious.
-
- **Bring humor into conversations.** Ask
  people, "What's the funniest thing that
  happened to you today? This week? In your
  life?"

Developing your sense of humor:
Take yourself less seriously

One essential characteristic that helps us
laugh is not taking ourselves too seriously. We've
all known the classic tight-jawed sourpuss who
takes everything with deathly seriousness and never
laughs at anything. No fun there!

Some events are clearly sad and not
occasions for laughter. But most events in life don't
carry an overwhelming sense of either sadness *or*
delight. They fall into the gray zone of ordinary
life–giving you the choice to laugh or not.

Ways to help yourself see the lighter side of life:

- **Laugh at yourself.** Share your embarrassing
  moments. The best way to take yourself less
  seriously is to talk about times when you
  took yourself too seriously.

- **Attempt to laugh at situations rather than bemoan them.** Look for the humor in a bad situation, and uncover the irony and absurdity of life. This will help improve your mood and the mood of those around you.

- **Surround yourself with reminders to lighten up.** Keep a toy on your desk or in your car. Put up a funny poster in your office. Choose a computer screensaver that makes you laugh. Frame photos of you and your family or friends having fun.

- **Keep things in perspective.** Many things in life are beyond your control—particularly the behavior of other people. While you might think taking the weight of the world on your shoulders is admirable, in the long run it's unrealistic, unproductive, unhealthy, and even egotistical.

- **Deal with your stress.** Stress is a major impediment to humor and laughter.

- **Pay attention to children and emulate them.** They are the experts on playing, taking life lightly, and laughing.

Checklist for lightening up

When you find yourself taken over by what seems to be a horrible problem, ask these questions:

- Is it really worth getting upset over?
- Is it worth upsetting others?
- Is it that important?
- Is it that bad?
- Is the situation irreparable?
- Is it really your problem?

Using humor and play to overcome challenges and enhance your life

The ability to laugh, play, and have fun with others not only makes life more enjoyable but also helps you solve problems, connect with others, and be more creative. People who incorporate humor and play into their daily lives find that it renews them and all of their relationships.

Life brings challenges that can either get the best of you or become playthings for your imagination. When you "become the problem" and take yourself too seriously, it can be hard to think outside the box and find new solutions. But when you play with the problem, you can often transform it into an opportunity for creative learning.

Playing with problems seems to come naturally to children. When they are confused or afraid, they make their problems into a game, giving them a sense of control and an opportunity to experiment with new solutions. Interacting with others in playful ways helps you retain this creative ability.

Humor is the ability to find joy and amusement in life, while laughter is the body's way of expressing what is found humorous.

They are a state of the mind, body and soul. Humor can improve your mind-spirit dimension of health by encouraging a positive, hopeful attitude. It gives a sense of perspective on problems in life and can help take your mind off discomforts and stress.

Humor also can benefit your social dimension of health, improving and strengthening relationships with friends and family

Ten Tips for Adding Humor to Your Life
by Carol Schlef, RNC, MSW, IBCLC

1. Start each day with a smile--even if you have to fake it!
2. Fit in five minutes of "mirth-ercise" daily, to stay humorously fit.
3. De-stress your life, by shaking off distress with a full minute of belly laughing.
4. Read at least one funny story, cartoon, or riddle daily.
5. Collect something child-like: funny buttons, Pez dispensers, practical jokes, balloons, silly glasses/masks, kaleidoscopes, etc.
6. Share a smile with at least three people every day.
7. Keep a journal: each night record at least three observations, events, or activities from your day that you can smile/laugh about.

8. Add color to your wardrobe. Buy at least one outlandish tie, scarf, tiebar or lapel pin, and wear it regularly--and proudly!
9. If you watch the nightly news, create a new, uplifting ending to ata least one news story.
10. Let your children (or your friends' children) see you modeling "fun", playful behavior at least once each week.

What is the greatest reward of being alive? Is it chocolate, sex, ice cream, tropical vacations, hugs from children, a perfect night's sleep, or the satisfaction of a job well done? A thousand people, a thousand different answers. But one supreme pleasure that spans all people is laughter.
Little can compare to the feeling of a deep, complete, heartfelt laughing spell. No matter your age, wealth, race, or living situation, life is good when laughter is frequent.

Life is also healthier. Research finds that humor can help you cope better with pain, enhance your immune system, reduce stress, even help you live longer. Laughter, doctors and psychologists agree, is an essential component of a healthy, happy life.

As Mark Twain once said, "Studying humor is like dissecting a frog — you may know a lot but you end up with a dead frog." Nonetheless, we're giving it a try.

Here are 19 tips for getting — or growing — your sense of humor, based partly on the idea that you can't be funny if you don't understand what funny is.

1. First, regain your smile. A smile and a laugh aren't the same thing, but they do live in the same neighborhood. Be sure to smile at simple pleasures — the sight of kids playing, a loved one or friend approaching, the successful completion of a task, the witnessing of something amazing or humorous. Smiles indicate that stress and the weight of the world haven't overcome you. If your day isn't marked by at least a few dozen, then you need to explore whether you are depressed or overly stressed.

2. Treat yourself to a comedy festival. Rent movies like *Meet the Parents; Young Frankenstein; Pee-Wee's Big Adventure; Monty Python and the Holy Grail; This Is Spinal Tap; Animal House; Blazing Saddles; Trading Places; Finding Nemo.* Reward yourself frequently with the gift of laughter, Hollywood style.

3. Recall several of the most embarrassing moments in your life. Then find the humor in them. Now practice telling stories describing them in a humorous way. It might take a little exaggeration or dramatization, but that's what good storytelling is all about. By revealing your vulnerable moments and being self-deprecating, you open yourself up much more to the humorous aspects of life.

4. Anytime something annoying and frustrating occurs, turn it on its head and find the humor. Sure, you can be angry at getting splashed with mud, stepping in dog poop, or inadvertently throwing a red towel in with the white laundry. In fact, that is probably the most normal response. But it doesn't accomplish anything other than to put you in a sour mood. Better to find a way to laugh at life's little annoyances. One way to do that: Think about it as if it happened to someone else, someone you like — or maybe someone you don't. In fact, keep running through the Rolodex in your head until you find the best person you can think of to put in your current predicament. Laugh at him, then laugh at yourself!

5. Read the comics every day and cut out the ones that remind you of your life. Post them on a bulletin board or the refrigerator or anywhere else you can see them frequently.

6. Sort through family photographs and write funny captions or one-liners to go with your favorites. When you need a pick-me-up, pull out the album.

7. Every night at dinner, make family members share one funny or even embarrassing moment of their day.

8. When a person offends you or makes you angry, respond with humor rather than hostility. For instance, if someone is always late, say, "Well, I'm glad you're not running an airline." Life is too short to turn every personal affront into a battle. However, if you are constantly offended by someone in particular, yes, take it seriously and take appropriate action. But for occasional troubles, or if nothing you do can change the person or situation, take the humor response.

9. Check out the Top 10 list archive from David Letterman. You can find it at cbs.com.

10. Spend 15 minutes a day having a giggling session. Here's how you do it: You and another person (partner, kid, friend, etc.) lie on the floor with your head on her stomach, and her head on another person's stomach and so on (the more people the better). The first person says, "Ha." The next person says, "Ha-ha." The third person says, "Ha-ha-ha." And so on. We guarantee you'll be laughing in no time.

11. Read the activity listings page in the newspaper and choose some laugh-inducing events to attend. It could be the circus, a movie, a stand-up comic, or a funny play. Sometimes it takes a professional to get you to regain your sense of humor.

12. Add an item to your daily to-do list: Find something humorous. Don't mark it off until you do it, suggests Jeanne Robertson, a humor expert and author of several books on the topic.

13. When you run into friends or coworkers, ask them to tell you one funny thing that has happened to them in the past couple of weeks. Become known as a person who wants to hear humorous true stories as opposed to an individual who prefers to hear gossip, suggests Robertson.

14. Find a humor buddy. This is someone you can call just to tell him something funny; someone who will also call you with funny stories of things he's seen or experienced, says Robertson.

15. Exaggerate and overstate problems. Making the situation bigger than life can help us to regain a humorous perspective, says Patty Wooten, R.N., an award-winning humorist and author of *Compassionate Laughter: Jest for the Health of It.* Cartoon caricatures, slapstick comedy, and clowning articles are all based on exaggeration, she notes.

16. Develop a silly routine to break a dark mood. It could be something as silly as speaking with a Swedish accent (unless you are Swedish, of course).

17. Create a humor environment. Have a ha-ha bulletin board where you only post funny sayings or signs, suggests Allen Klein, an award-winning professional speaker and author of *The Healing Power of Humor*. His favorite funny sign: "Never wrestle with a pig. You both get dirty, and the pig likes it."

18. Experiment with jokes. Learn one simple joke each week and spread it around. One of Klein's favorites relates to his baldness: "What do you call a line of rabbits walking backward? A receding hare line."

19. Focus humor on yourself. "Because of my lack of hair," Klein says, "I tell people that I'm a former expert on how to cure baldness."

NOW GO OUT AND MAKE EVERY HOUR IN YOUR LIFE –

Made in the USA
San Bernardino, CA
05 October 2013